CARS

Author:

Ian Graham was born
in Belfast in 1953. He studied
applied physics at The City
University, London, and took a
postgraduate diploma in
journalism, specialising in
science and technology
journalism. After four years
as a magazine editor, he
became a freelance author and
journalist. Since then, he has
written more than one hundred
children's non-fiction books and
numerous magazine articles.

Artist:

Mark Bergin was born
in Hastings, England, in 1961.
He studied at Eastbourne
College of Art, and since 1983
he has specialised in historical
reconstructions as well as
aviation and maritime subjects.
He lives in Bexhill-on-Sea with
his wife and three children.

Consultant:

Monica Hughes
is an experienced educational
advisor and author of more than
one hundred books for young
children. She has been head
teacher of a primary school,
primary advisory teacher, and
senior lecturer in early
childhood education.

Editor:

Stephen Haynes

Editorial Assistant:

Mark Williams

**PAPER FROM
SUSTAINABLE
FORESTS**

This book is adapted from
Cars by Ian Graham, created,
designed and produced by The
Salariya Book Company and
published by Hodder Wayland in
MM in the Fast Forward series.

SALARIYA

Published in Great Britain MMIX by
Book House, an imprint of
The Salariya Book Company Ltd
25 Marlborough Place, Brighton, BNI IUB
www.salariya.com
www.book-house.co.uk

PB ISBN 978-1-906714-53-6

A CIP Catalogue record for this book is available
from the British Library.

Printed and bound in China.
Printed on paper from sustainable sources.

Visit our websites at **www.salariya.com** or
www.book-house.co.uk
for **free** electronic versions of:
You Wouldn't Want to be an Egyptian Mummy!
You Wouldn't Want to be a Roman Gladiator!
Avoid Joining Shackleton's Polar Expedition!
Avoid Sailing on a 19th-Century Whaling Ship!

CARS

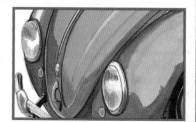

Written by

IAN GRAHAM

Illustrated by

MARK BERGIN

Created and designed by

DAVID SALARIYA

Contents

The First Automobiles

The first 'horseless carriages' were powered by steam. They were noisy, slow and dirty. They were sometimes dangerous – the boilers could explode. The petrol engine was invented in 1885. It made the car into a much better form of transport.

▲ Italy, around 1495: Leonardo da Vinci drew a clockwork tricycle.

◀ France, 1769: Nicolas-Joseph Cugnot's steam tractor reached 3.6 kph (2.2 mph).

▼ England, 1826: Sir Goldsworthy Gurney built a steam carriage. These carriages had to stop about every 6 km (4 miles) to fill their boilers with water.

▲ Scotland, 29 July 1834: A steam carriage exploded. It was the first fatal motor accident.

LONDON AND BATH

| 1 | 2 | 3 | 4 | Spark plug
Valve
Cylinder
Piston
Crankshaft |

Fuel and air in | **Piston** moves up | **Spark plug** fires | Burnt gases out

▲ Most car engines work in four steps.

▲ Germany, 1885: Karl Benz built the first petrol-engined car. It had three wheels and a one-cylinder engine. Its top speed was 15 kph (9 mph).

▲ USA, 1908:
The Ford Model T had a four-cylinder engine. It had a top speed of 65 kph (40 mph). Its low price made it popular. More than 15 million cars of this type were sold.

▶ Germany, 1945: The Volkswagen 'Beetle' became the most popular car ever built. More than 21 million were sold.

Designing a Car

Computers and robots make it quicker to design new cars. Computer animations show what the car will look like from all directions. Robots can be programmed to produce identical cars 24 hours a day.

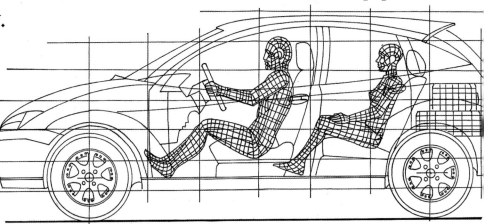

▲ Most designs start with a sketch on paper.

► This drawing shows how much space is inside the car.

◄ Computer Aided Design (CAD) allows designers to check that all the parts fit and move properly.

► A computer-controlled machine makes a full-size mock-up out of clay or polystyrene.

COMPUTER MODELLING

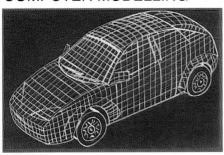

▲ This type of 3D drawing is called a 'wireframe' image.

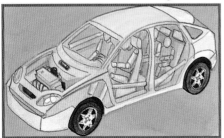

▲ Interior details are added to give this X-ray view.

▲ Colour, texture and shadows are added. This picture now looks like a photo of a real car.

▶ Cars are tested in a wind tunnel to see how air flows around them.

◀ A few **prototypes** are built by hand. These are driven on test-tracks. Any problems can then be fixed.

▶ Finally, the car goes into production. The steel body shell is welded by robots.

▼ More robots paint the car. Then the engine is put in and the wheels are fitted. The seats and windows are fitted last of all.

The Land Speed Record

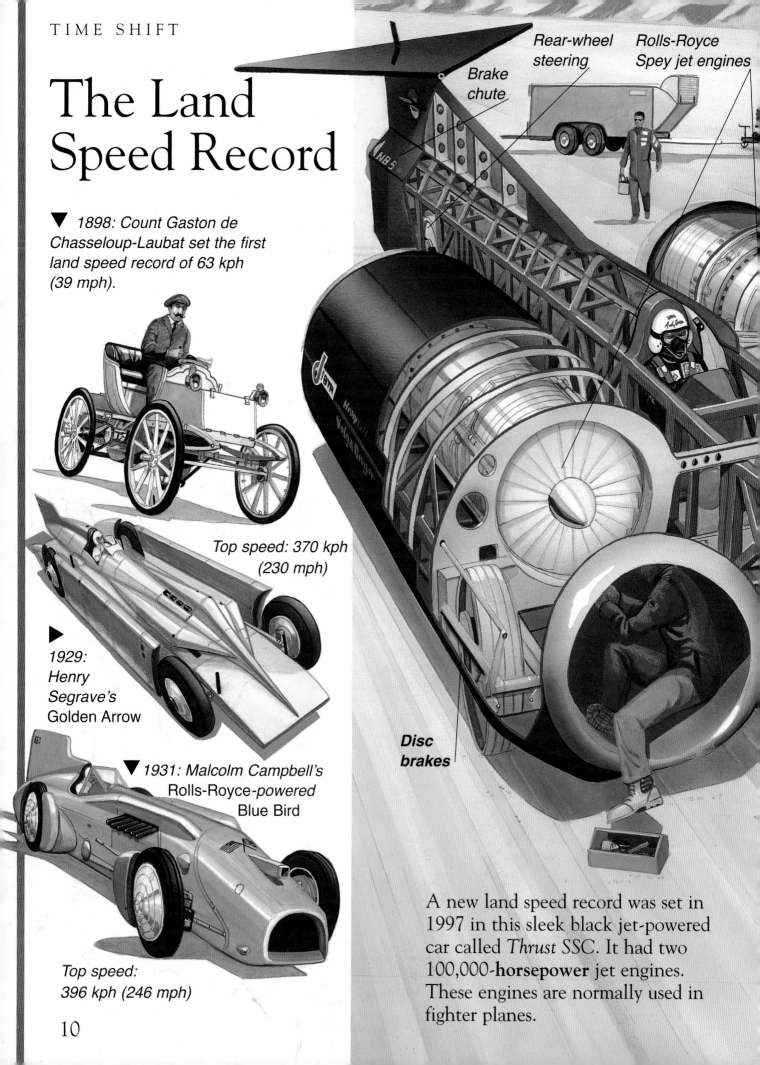

▼ 1898: Count Gaston de Chasseloup-Laubat set the first land speed record of 63 kph (39 mph).

Top speed: 370 kph (230 mph)

▶ 1929: Henry Segrave's Golden Arrow

▼ 1931: Malcolm Campbell's Rolls-Royce-powered Blue Bird

Top speed: 396 kph (246 mph)

Brake chute

Rear-wheel steering

Rolls-Royce Spey jet engines

Disc brakes

A new land speed record was set in 1997 in this sleek black jet-powered car called *Thrust SSC*. It had two 100,000-**horsepower** jet engines. These engines are normally used in fighter planes.

Thrust SSC blasts its way across the Black Rock Desert in the United States. On 15 October 1997 it reached a record 1,228 kph (763 mph). The Black Rock Desert is so big and flat that a car can **accelerate** to more than 1,000 kph. When *Thrust SSC* reached **supersonic** speed the spectators heard the tell-tale sonic boom.

Electric and steam-driven cars were the first to break land speed records. By the 1960s cars with jet engines could go even faster.

▼ 1964: Donald Campbell's gas-turbine-engined Bluebird

Top speed: 648 kph (403 mph)

▲ 1965: Art Arfons's Green Monster *jet-car* 922 kph (573 mph)

▲ Gary Gabelich's rocket-powered Blue Flame. Top speed: 995 kph (618 mph)

▼ 1983: Thrust 2, driven by Richard Noble

Top speed: 1,019 kph (633 mph)

13

Supercars & Muscle Cars

The fastest cars on the road are supercars and muscle cars.

◀ Chrysler Viper (USA)

8-litre, 10-cylinder engine; top speed 250 kph (155 mph)

▼ Lamborghini Diablo VT (Italy)

5.7-litre, 12-cylinder engine; top speed more than 320 kph (200 mph)

▼ Jaguar XJ220 (UK): *3.5-litre, 6-cylinder engine; top speed 350 kph (217 mph)*

Fire-resistant suit
(in case of fuel spills)

Tyre
carrier

Tyre
changer

'Lollipop'
stop–go
sign

The pit
crew crowds
[aroun]d a Formula 1 car
[when it stops during a race to change its] **[tyres]stop.** They
[change the whe]els and refuel
[the car in just a few s]econds.

Jack
man

**FORMULA 1
CHAMPIONS**

1950s

Juan
Manuel Fangio

Stirling Moss

1960s

Jim Clark

Jackie Stewart

1970s

Niki Lauda

1980s

Ayrton Senna

Alain Prost

1990s–2000s

Michael Schumacher

Sports Stars

Some racing cars are the same shape as ordinary cars. They are sometimes called 'tin tops'. Most races are won by the first car to cross the finish line.

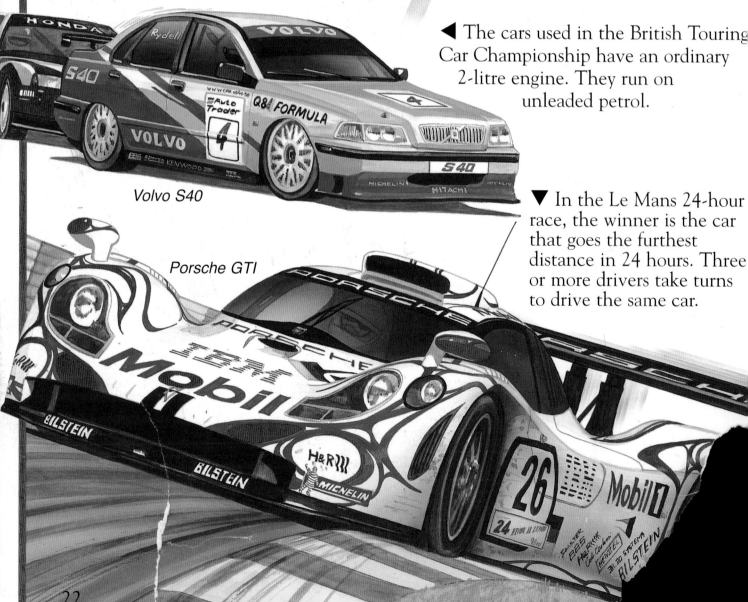

Volvo S40

Porsche GTI

◀ The cars used in the British Touring Car Championship have an ordinary 2-litre engine. They run on unleaded petrol.

▼ In the Le Mans 24-hour race, the winner is the car that goes the furthest distance in 24 hours. Three or more drivers take turns to drive the same car.

◄ Here, Jeff Burton and Jeff Gordon battle for the lead during the Daytona 500 motor race, which is held in February each year.

▼ Rally cars race against time, not each other. Each car sets off one minute after the car before. In stage rallies, the cars are driven at high-speeds across forest tracks and rough ground. The navigator warns the driver of what is ahead.

Driver Carlos Sainz and navigator Luis Moya of Team Toyota Corolla

23

Sheer Luxury

Luxury cars like this Rolls-Royce Silver Seraph are built to give a very smooth, almost silent ride.

▲ The Cadillac DeVille Concours has an electronic 'brain'. The wipers start automatically when it rains. The front seats can give you a massage!

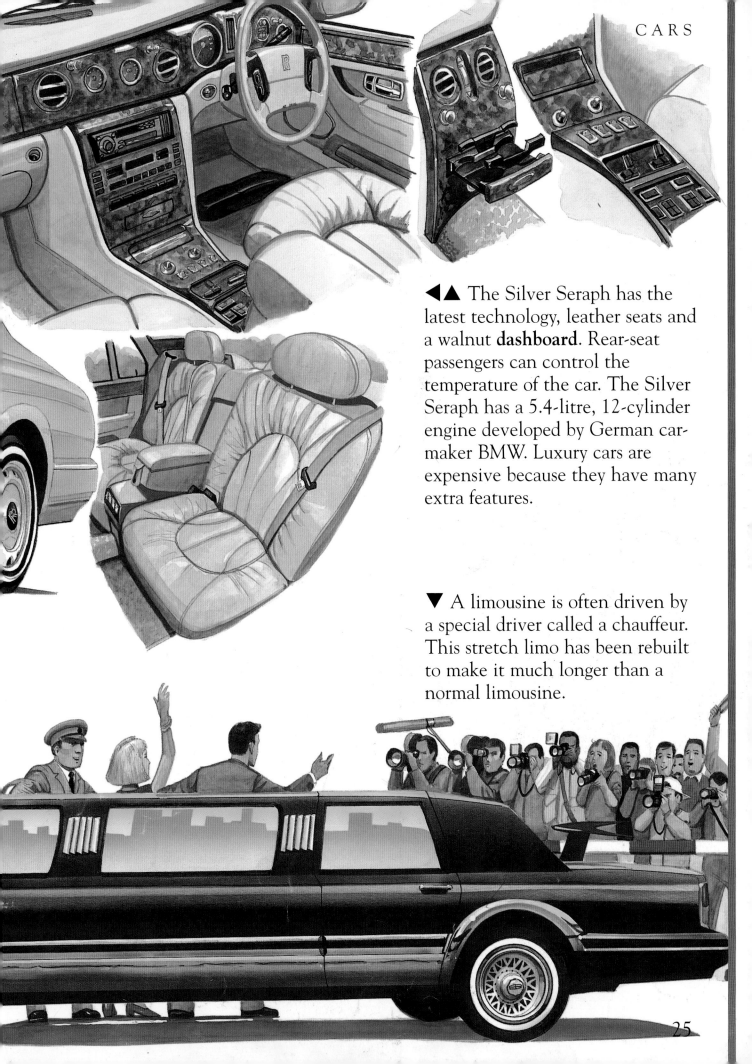

◄▲ The Silver Seraph has the latest technology, leather seats and a walnut **dashboard**. Rear-seat passengers can control the temperature of the car. The Silver Seraph has a 5.4-litre, 12-cylinder engine developed by German car-maker BMW. Luxury cars are expensive because they have many extra features.

▼ A limousine is often driven by a special driver called a chauffeur. This stretch limo has been rebuilt to make it much longer than a normal limousine.

Car Safety

Headlights, anti-lock brakes and eye-level brake lights help to prevent accidents. Seat belts and air bags protect passengers if an accident happens.

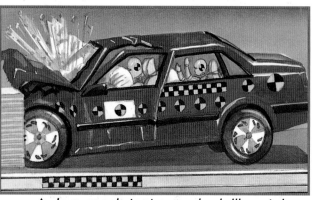

▲ *In a crash test a car is deliberately crashed. Dummies show what would happen to real people in a car crash.*

Brake lights warn ▶ people that a car is slowing down or stopping.

▲ *The grooves in tyres squeeze water out from under them. This stops the car skating over the water.*

Anti-lock brakes stop the tyres from losing grip and causing the car to skid.

Safety-glass windscreen

Deformable bumper

Hazard light

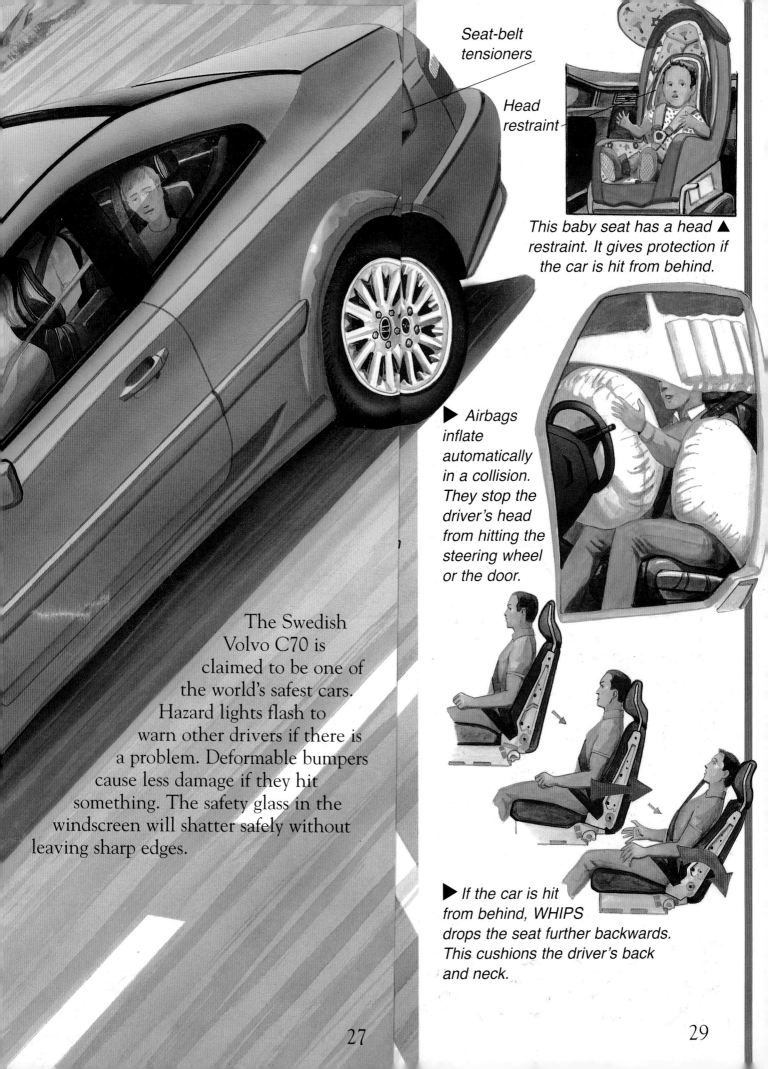

Seat-belt
tensioners

Head
restraint

This baby seat has a head ▲
restraint. It gives protection if
the car is hit from behind.

► Airbags
inflate
automatically
in a collision.
They stop the
driver's head
from hitting the
steering wheel
or the door.

The Swedish
Volvo C70 is
claimed to be one of
the world's safest cars.
Hazard lights flash to
warn other drivers if there is
a problem. Deformable bumpers
cause less damage if they hit
something. The safety glass in the
windscreen will shatter safely without
leaving sharp edges.

► If the car is hit
from behind, WHIPS
drops the seat further backwards.
This cushions the driver's back
and neck.

27

29

Useful Words

Accelerate
Go faster. The pedal a driver presses to make a car go faster is called the accelerator.

Carbon fibre
A strong, lightweight material made from very thin fibres of almost pure carbon.

Crankshaft
A kind of axle inside a petrol or diesel engine, which is turned by the pistons as they move up and down. It is connected to the gears that drive the wheels.

Cylinder
A metal tube inside a car's engine, inside which the fuel is burned. Most car engines have four or more cylinders.

Dashboard (or fascia)
The control panel in front of a car's driver.

Deformable bumper
A bumper made from a soft material that changes shape when it touches something. It is safer than a hard metal bumper in accidents involving pedestrians or cyclists.

Disc brakes
Brakes that slow the car down by using hard, rough pads to grip a steel disc fixed to each road wheel.

Fuel
A liquid such as petrol or diesel oil that is burned inside a car engine.

Horsepower
A measurement of the power of an engine.

Piston
A plunger that slides up and down inside an engine's cylinder, turning the crankshaft.

Pit stop
A visit to the pits (garages at the side of a motor-racing track) by a racing car during a race to have its tyres changed and/or to fill up with fuel.

Pneumatic
Powered by air pressure.

Prototype
The first model of a car. It is tested to make sure that everything works properly before more cars are made.

Spark plug
A device that makes an electric spark to burn the fuel inside the cylinder and move the piston.

Supersonic
Faster than the speed of sound.

Valve
A device that allows fuel and air to flow into and out of a cylinder.

Milestones

1769 The first motor vehicle, a steam tractor, is built in France by Nicolas-Joseph Cugnot.

1885 Karl Benz builds the first petrol-driven motor car.

1891 The first electric car, called the Electrobat, is built by Morris and Salom in Philadelphia, USA.

1893 Rudolf Diesel invents the diesel engine.

1895 André and Edouard Michelin make the first pneumatic (air-filled) tyres for cars. They are based on John Boyd Dunlop's invention of the pneumatic tyre.

1902 Disc brakes are invented for use in military vehicles.

1908 The Model T Ford goes into mass production in Detroit, USA.

1911 The first self-starter for automobiles is invented. It replaces the starting handle.

1918 A third (amber) light is added to red–green traffic lights.

1919 Hydraulic brakes (operated by oil pressure) are developed for automobiles.

1921 The first motorway is built, in Germany.

1930 Cedric Dicksee develops a diesel engine for road vehicles.

1947 Raymond Loewy designs the first modern streamlined car, made by Studebaker.

1950 The Formula 1 World Motor Racing Championship begins.

1951 The US car maker Chrysler fits its cars with power-assisted steering.

1953 A Jaguar car with disc brakes wins the Le Mans 24-hour race. This leads to the use of disc brakes in ordinary cars.

1961 The five-door car, or hatchback, is introduced by Renault.

1981 The air bag is invented by Daimler-Benz.

2008 At 23, British driver Lewis Hamilton becomes the youngest ever Formula 1 World Champion.

2008 US company Terrafugia reveals a prototype 'roadable aircraft'. This two-seater aeroplane can be converted into a car in just 15 seconds.

Index